The ABCs of Law

Written by Raamin Mostaghimi

Edited by Varun Bhartia

Illustrated by Kyle Navaluna

For our spouses, who tolerate every single one of our terrible lawyer jokes with remarkable resolve

Copyright © 2018 Very Young Professionals Publishing
www.veryyoungprofessionals.com

All rights reserved

ISBN-13:
978-1-7325217-2-8

A is for **attorney**

*An **attorney**, or lawyer, is someone who gives legal advice and represents other people in court. You have to go to school for a long time and take a really hard test to become an **attorney**!*

B is for **bar exam**

*Before you can become a lawyer, first you have to pass the **bar exam** in your state - so don't forget to study!*

C is for **contingency fee**

If you don't have enough money to hire a lawyer, you might find one that works for a **contingency fee** - you'll just pay them a lot of your earnings after you win.

D is for **defendant**

*When you're a **defendant** in a case, that means you're being accused of doing something wrong! Don't worry - you're still innocent until proven guilty.*

E is for **evidence**

A good lawyer knows that to win their cases, they need lots of **evidence** - otherwise they have no proof!

F is for **felony**

If someone commits a **felony**, they could go to jail for a looooooong time.

G is for guilty

If a judge or jury decides that you've done the thing you're accused of, they will declare that you are **guilty**.

H is for **hearsay**

A lot people think **hearsay** counts as evidence, but really it's just gossip.

I is for **injunction**

When the court issues you an **injunction**, you have to stop doing whatever you're doing - and if you don't, you could be in big trouble!

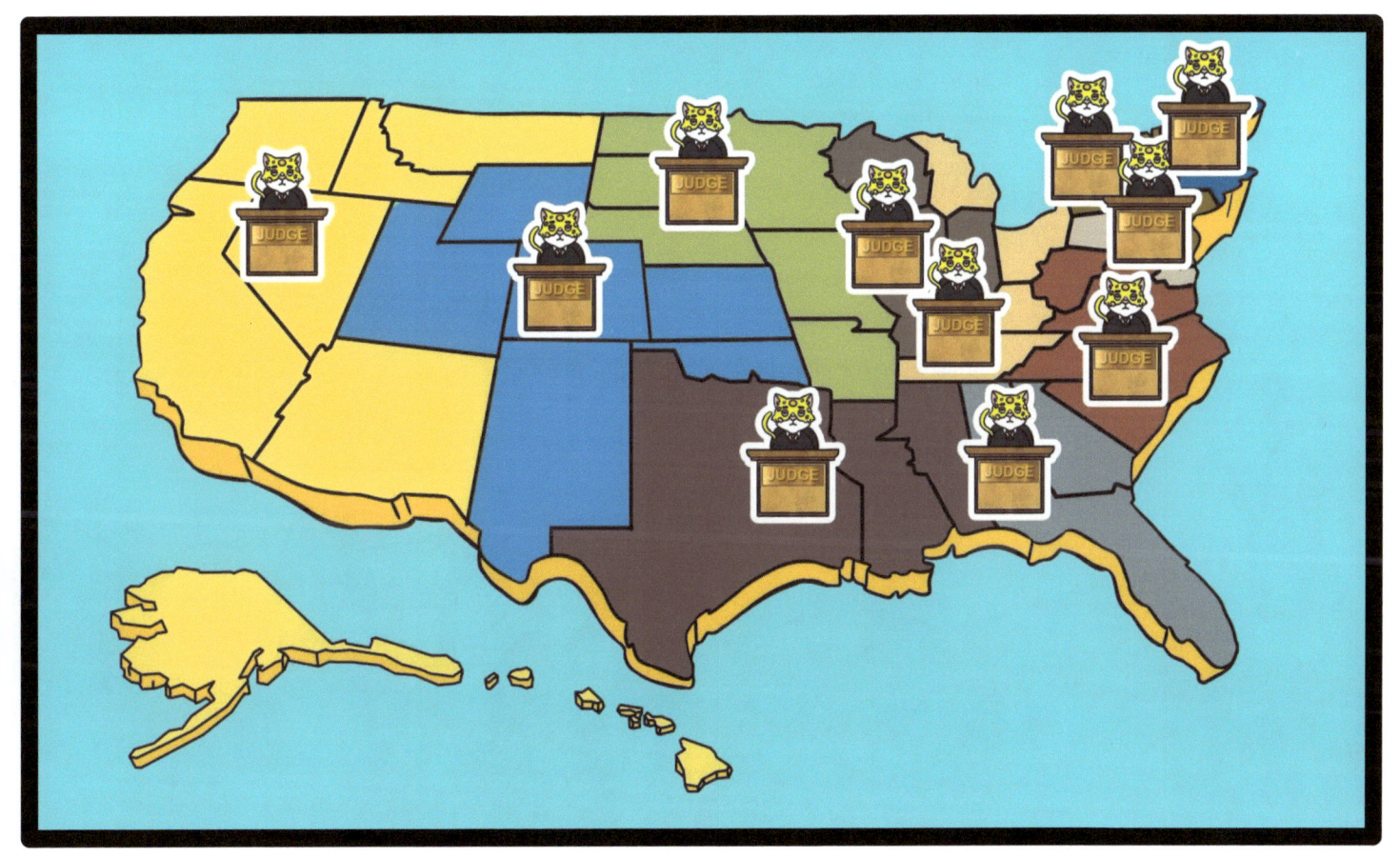

J is for **jurisdiction**

*You can't just go to any court anywhere if you want to sue somebody – you have to pick the one with the right **jurisdiction** so it can hear your case.*

K is for **contracts**

Weird, right?? When they need an abbreviation for **contracts**, most lawyers and law students will use the letter **K**.

L is for **libel**

*Printing things that you know are lies about somebody isn't just mean – it's also a crime called **libel**.*

M is for **motion**

Lawyers can't just ask judges to do things for them – they have to make formal **motions** to the court.

N is for **negligence**

*Sometimes, even just forgetting to do something you were supposed to do can be a crime - it's called **negligence**.*

O is for **objection**

If a lawyer doesn't like something that opposing counsel is saying in court, they might dramatically shout "**Objection!!**"

P is for plaintiff

*When you're the person who originally files a complaint with the court, you're called a **plaintiff**.*

Q is for *qui tam*

One good way to make some money is to help the government file a **qui tam** lawsuit – that means you help them win their case in exchange for some of the relief.

R is for relief

If you win a lawsuit, you might get **relief** at the end – which could be money, property, or some other valuable thing.

S is for **standing**

Not just anybody can file a lawsuit! First you need to prove that you have **standing** - that you suffered an injury that can be corrected by the court, among other things.

T is for **tort**

If you break a civil law, you haven't committed a crime - you've committed a **tort** instead.

U is for **unjust enrichment**

A person who keeps money that shouldn't be theirs is **unjustly enriching** themselves.

V is for *voir dire*

If a lawyer doesn't like the jury for a case, they can change some of the members through a process called **voir dire.**

W is for witness

You witness hundreds of things every single day - anything you see! If you're asked to be a **witness** in court, you'll have to promise to tell the truth.

X is for eXtradition

If a person commits a crime in America and then runs away to Canada, they can be **extradited** back when they get caught.

Y is for Your Honor

Unless you want to get thrown out of court, you had better show the judge respect by calling them "**Your Honor**".

Z is for **zealous**

Every lawyer is supposed to be a **zealous** advocate for the rights of their clients - they have to do everything ethical within their power to win.